Listen! You may not see them. But you
can hear them. The sounds of insects fill the night air.

5

The insect world is alive with strange sounds, beautiful colors, and fascinating creatures.

Thread-waisted wasp

Butterfly

How busy the insects are! Watch them closely as they work, fight, and hunt. There's so much to see.

Stag beetle

Oak gall wasp

Insects are found almost everywhere on Earth. There are many, many kinds of insects. Over a million types of insects are known. Some scientists believe there are millions more to discover.

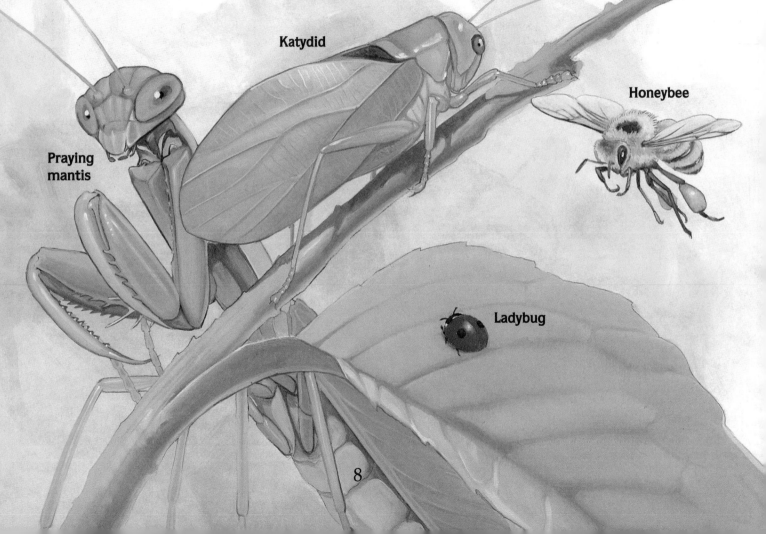

Katydid

Honeybee

Praying
mantis

Ladybug

8

Insects come in many shapes and sizes. Some, like the flea, are so tiny you need a magnifying glass to see them clearly. Others, such as the tropical walking stick, are nearly a foot (.3 meter) long.

Walking stick

Flea

Some insects have special oarlike legs for swimming.
Others have powerful legs for jumping or digging.
Most insects have strong wings for flying.

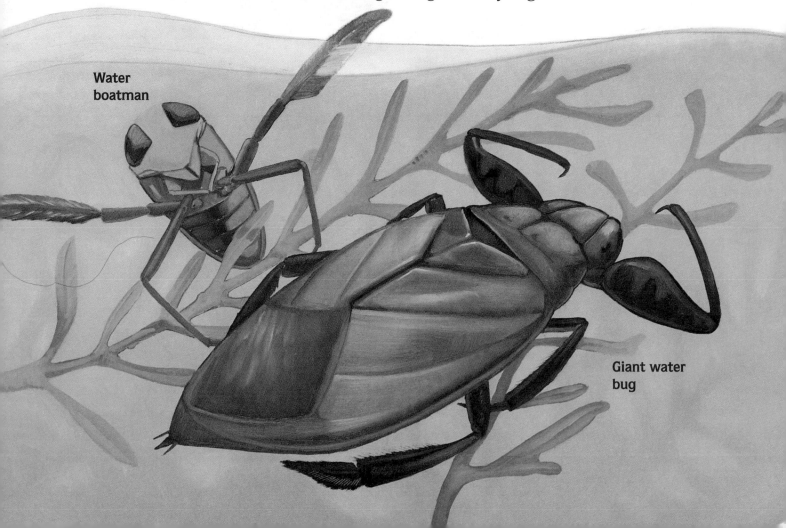

Water
boatman

Giant water
bug

Insects live in many different places. Water bugs and dragonflies live in or near water. Some insects, such as ants, may live underground. Others—for example, butterflies—spend a lot of time in the air, flying long distances.

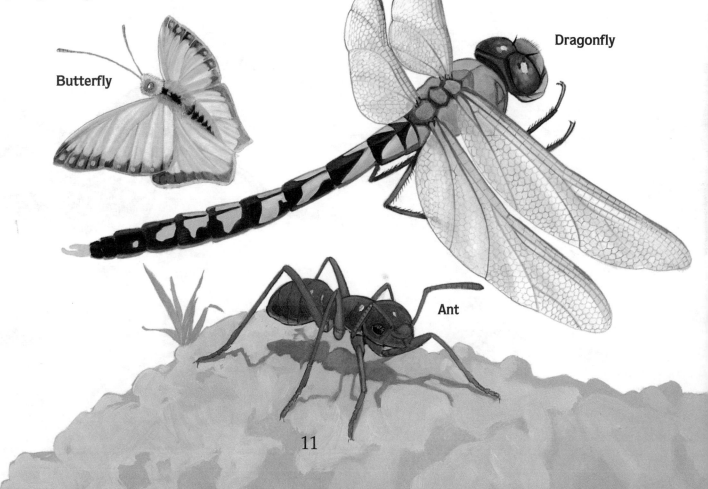

Butterfly

Dragonfly

Ant

No other group in the animal kingdom has as many different colors and patterns on their bodies as the insects do. Some are brightly colored with red, blue, yellow, orange, or green. Some have stripes and dots. Others look like sand, earth, leaves, bark, or twigs. They blend in with their surroundings in order to hide from their enemies or to surprise their prey.

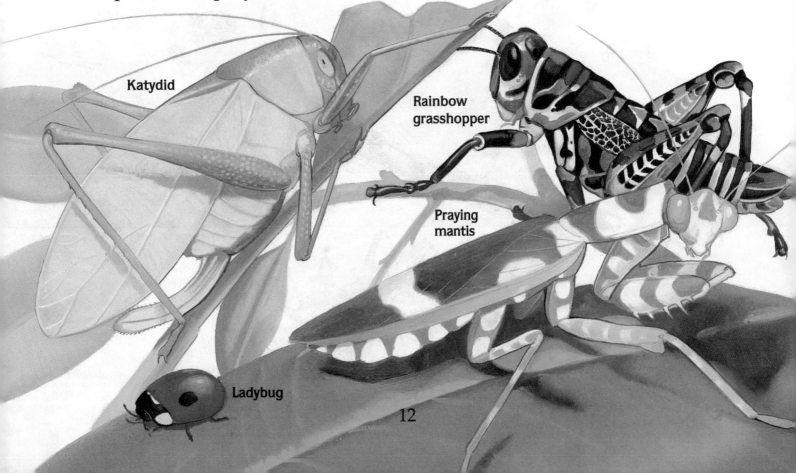

Katydid

Rainbow grasshopper

Praying mantis

Ladybug

12

No matter how they look, however, all insects are alike in certain ways. All insects have six legs. They also all have three main parts to their bodies. Most insects have wings and a pair of feelers called *antennae* (an-TEN-ee) on the head for smelling and touching. In addition, all insects start life as a small egg.

Unlike you, an insect does not have a skeleton inside its body. Instead, it has a shell outside its body to protect it. As its body grows larger, the insect loses its too-small shell, growing a new and larger shell to fit it.

Polyphemus moth

The three main parts of an insect's body are the *head*, the *thorax* (THOR-aks), and the *abdomen* (AB-duh-men). On the head are the antennae, the eyes, and the mouth. The middle section is the thorax. Legs and wings are connected to the thorax. The abdomen is the back section. Food is digested in the abdomen.

Wings (4)

Abdomen

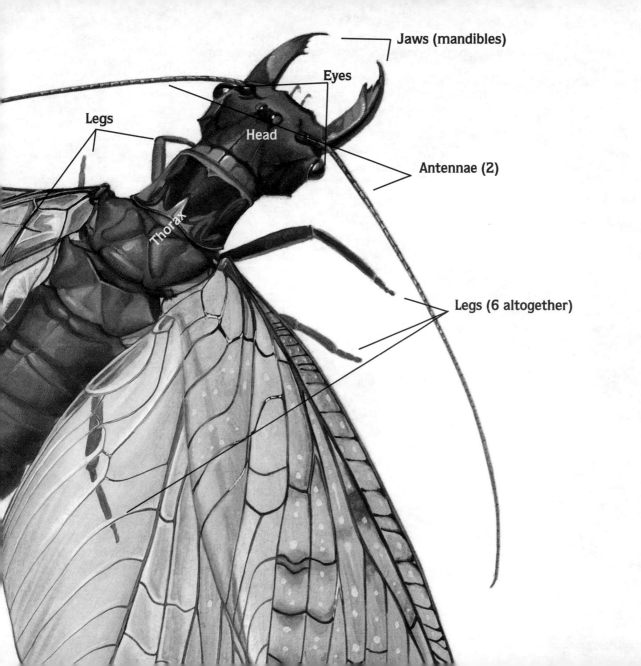

Jaws (mandibles)

Eyes

Legs

Head

Antennae (2)

Thorax

Legs (6 altogether)

An *entomologist* (en-tuh-MAH-luh-jist) is a scientist who studies insects and tries to learn more about their habits, diet, growth, habitats, and relationships.

Some of the most interesting insects are *social* insects. Social insects live in groups. They work together, sharing homes called *colonies*. In some ways, social insects are like a family or a small community. Ants, termites, and some kinds of bees are social insects.

Certain kinds of ants build their colonies underground. First, they dig tunnels from the top of the ground that lead down to the colony. Then the ants dig the special rooms of the colony.

Soldier

Queen

18

Each ant in the colony has a particular job to do. The queen ant lays all the eggs. There are many worker ants. All the workers are females. Some workers are soldiers, who must guard the colony. Some are nurses, who take care of the eggs. Other workers clean the rooms, while others hunt for food. Usually, males are present only at certain seasons. Their sole purpose is to mate with the queen or with the queens of other colonies.

Nurse

Eggs

Worker

Honeybees are also social insects. They live and work together in a colony called a *hive*. One queen lays all the eggs. The drones are males. They mate with the queen or with queens that are starting new colonies. Female workers do the work of the hive and get nectar from flowers to make honey.

Worker bees

Bee at center returns to hive. The "pollen baskets" on its legs are full of pollen.

A great many insects are not social. They live alone most of the time. These sorts of insects must find their own food. They must fight their own battles—sometimes life-and-death battles. Crickets, beetles, mosquitoes, and grasshoppers are these kinds of insects.

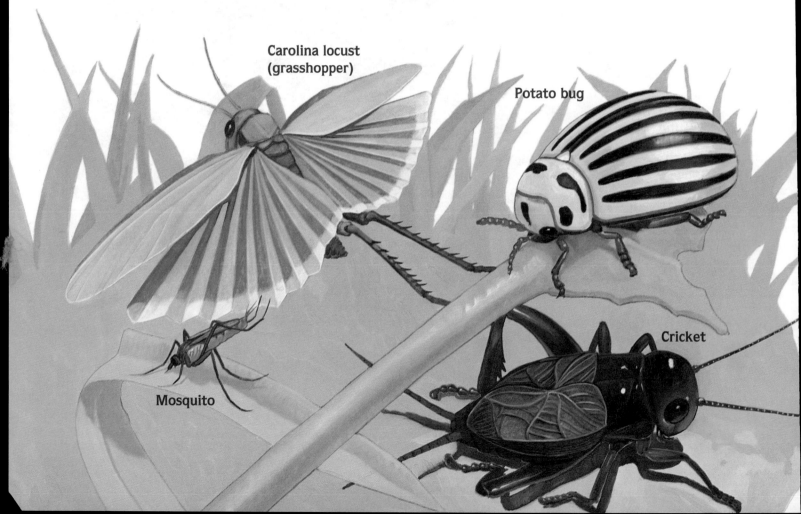

Carolina locust
(grasshopper)

Potato bug

Cricket

Mosquito

Life in the insect world is a constant struggle for survival. Most insects live less than a year. For them, life lasts one season at most. Even for insects that are able to live more than a year, there is constant danger. Such an insect may be eaten by another insect or animal. Disease may strike, or the insect may be killed by a person. In addition, if the weather is bad, plants that the insect feeds upon may die, and the insect will starve.

Male stag beetles fighting for territory

Insects grow into adults in stages. Some insects grow simply from eggs to small versions of the adult insects they will become. As this sort of insect molts, losing its too-small shell, it grows. Little by little, it becomes an adult.

Adult cicada

Other insects grow in stages that involve dramatic changes. The process of changing from an egg to an adult insect is called *metamorphosis* (meh-ta-MORE-fuh-sis).

The adult cicada, shown at far left, has changed dramatically during metamorphosis. It has just emerged from its former skin (near left). At first, the cicada's wings are wet and crumpled. After its wings dry and straighten out, the cicada will fly away.

Some insects go through metamorphosis in three stages. They start as an *egg*. Then they develop into something called a *nymph*. During this stage, the nymph may or may not look like its parents. The third and last stage is the *adult* stage.

Dragonflies, mayflies, chinch bugs, crickets, and grasshoppers are some of the insects that go through metamorphosis in three stages.

Dragonfly

Adult

Egg

Nymph

26

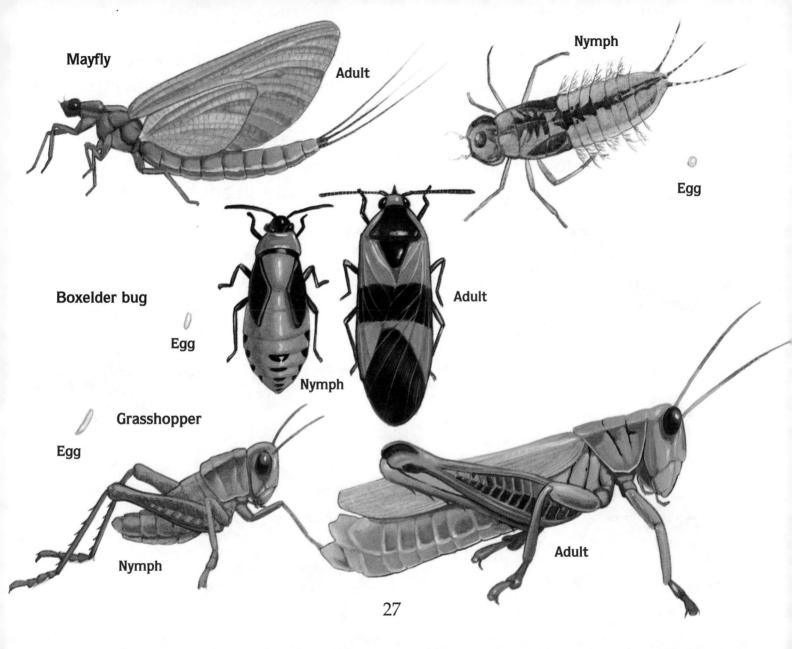

Mayfly

Adult

Nymph

Egg

Boxelder bug

Egg

Nymph

Adult

Grasshopper

Egg

Nymph

Adult

The female cricket, for instance, lays her eggs in the ground. When the eggs hatch, tiny crickets, which are the nymphs, appear. A nymph starts to eat. Soon, its body is ready to grow. The *molting* process begins—the nymph's outside shell splits and falls away. The new shell stretches to a larger size, and so the insect is able to grow. After several changes, the nymph finally develops into an adult cricket.

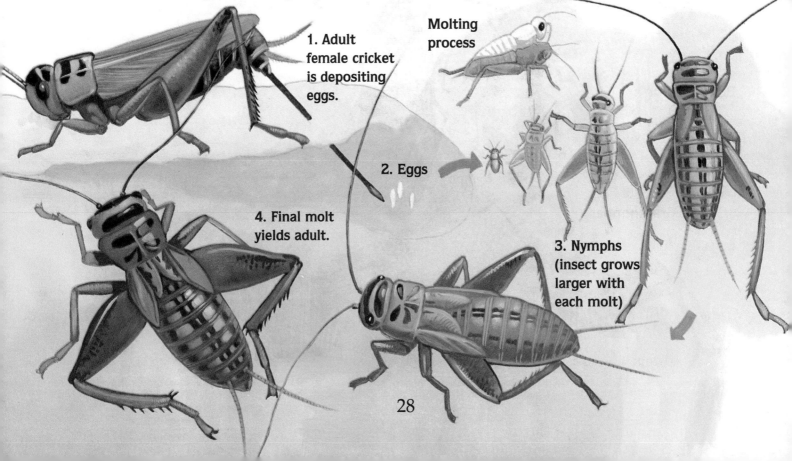

1. Adult female cricket is depositing eggs.

Molting process

2. Eggs

4. Final molt yields adult.

3. Nymphs (insect grows larger with each molt)

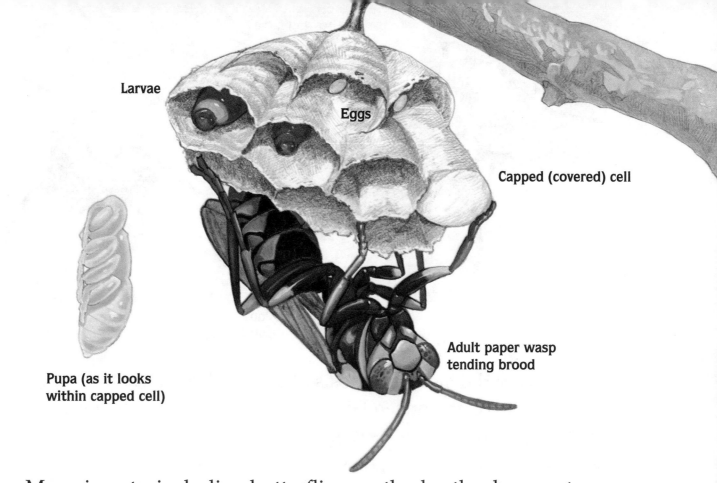

Larvae

Eggs

Capped (covered) cell

Adult paper wasp
tending brood

Pupa (as it looks
within capped cell)

Many insects, including butterflies, moths, beetles, bees, ants, and wasps, go through metamorphosis in four stages. This is called *complete metamorphosis.* The four stages include *egg, larva, pupa,* and *adult.*

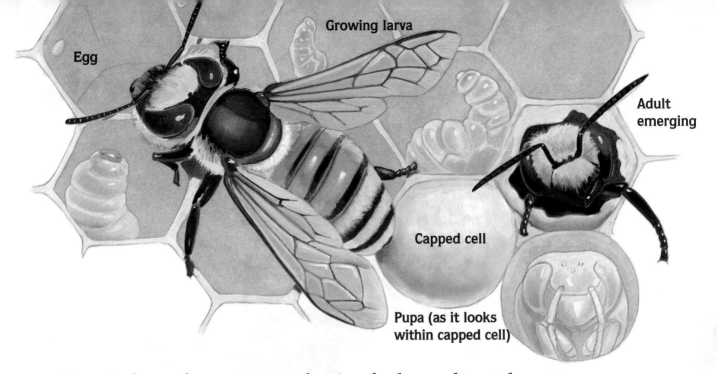

Egg

Growing larva

Adult emerging

Capped cell

Pupa (as it looks within capped cell)

Here is how the metamorphosis of a honeybee takes place. In the hive, the queen lays eggs in the cells of a honeycomb. In each egg, a creature starts to grow. It is a wormlike larva.

After three days, the egg hatches, and a worker feeds the larva honey and pollen. After five days, the worker puts a wax top over the cell. The larva is growing and changing inside. It becomes a pupa. After twenty-one days, a grown bee bites through the wax and crawls out of the cell.

For butterflies and moths, life also starts in the egg stage. Before long, the wormlike larva, which is called a *caterpillar*, hatches. It looks nothing like the butterfly or moth it will become.

The larva needs food. It eats and grows, and eats and grows. Then, when it is ready, the larva stops eating and gets ready to rest. It will now become a pupa. The larva spins a cocoon, which serves as a protective covering for the pupa. Inside, a great change is taking place. Then, one day, the covering splits or cracks open— and an adult insect emerges!

White-lined sphinx moth

Caterpillar

Pupa

Look closely at the larva of the monarch butterfly as it crawls upon a leaf. As the larva eats milkweed leaves and grows, it also molts, shedding its too-tight skin. Some caterpillars become more colorful with each molt. The monarch caterpillar has rings of white, yellow, and black on its shiny skin.

Monarch
caterpillar
(larva)

Milkweed leaves

32

When the monarch caterpillar is ready to stop eating, it attaches itself, upside down, to a branch or leaf by spinning a sticky silk thread. Now it is ready to enter the pupal stage. The pupal stage begins with a final molt. The caterpillar loses its bright colors and its many tiny legs.

Chrysalis
(pupa is inside)

The old skin slides off and falls to the ground. The monarch is now protected in a green sac called a *chrysalis* (KRIH-suh-liss). Inside the chrysalis, the pupa is turning into a butterfly.

Then, about twelve days later, the chrysalis cracks open. A beautiful butterfly emerges. At first, its wings are wet and wrinkled. When the wings dry, something wonderful happens. The adult butterfly is ready to take to the air!

Newly emerged adult

But for the monarchs that have emerged in late summer, there is much to do. As the summer ends, the monarchs of North America begin their seasonal journey south to find warmer weather. This kind of journey is called *migration*. Some monarchs will travel 2,000 miles (3,200 kilometers) looking for warmer weather. They travel by day and rest at night.

Adult monarch

The return journey back north when spring comes is hard for the monarchs. They are weak and tired. Most die along the way before completing the journey.

As they travel north, monarchs lay their eggs on the leaves of milkweed plants. When the eggs hatch, the caterpillars will eat the leaves of the milkweed.

After the caterpillars mature into butterflies, they continue the journey north. When winter approaches, the new generation of monarchs heads south, just as the generation before them did a year earlier.

The monarch is just one of many beautiful butterflies. Others include the viceroy, the zebra swallowtail, the blue night butterfly, the cabbage butterfly, and the zebra longwing.

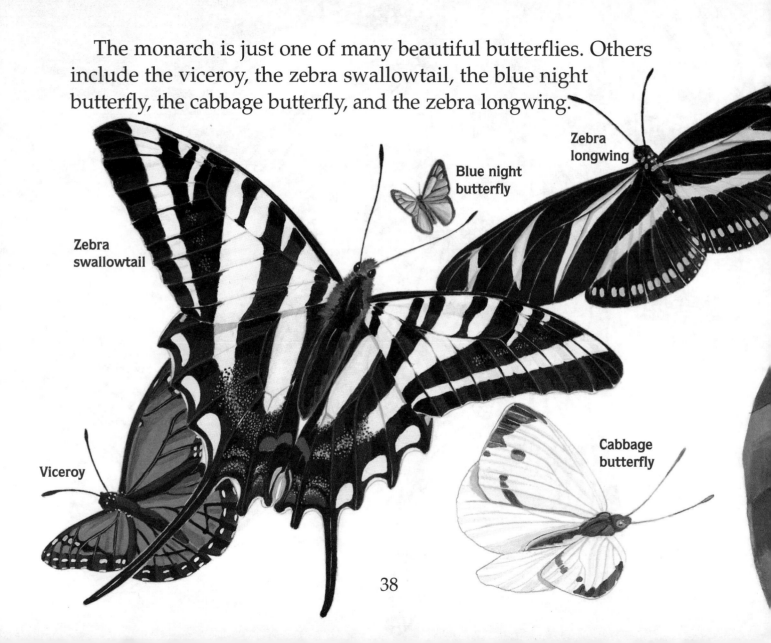

Zebra longwing

Blue night butterfly

Zebra swallowtail

Viceroy

Cabbage butterfly

The world of insects is filled with intriguing sights. Watch the fireflies at work at night. A firefly has a special organ in its abdomen that makes a glowing light. This flashing light is used to attract a mate.

Pennsylvania firefly

The insect world is also filled with strange sounds. Listen to the cricket chirping. The male cricket is the musician. He makes his chirping sound by rubbing his wings together. His purpose is also to attract a mate.

Cricket

Some insects are helpful to people. Others are harmful. Locusts, aphids, weevils, and Japanese beetles eat and damage crops. Lice, fleas, and mosquitoes and other flies can carry disease.

Locust
(Lubber
grasshopper)

Fly

Japanese
beetle

Rose
weevil

Aphids

Flea

Moths can also be harmful. Some, such as the hungry larva of the gypsy moth, can destroy trees. But other moths are helpful to people. They spin soft thread used to make the material we call silk.

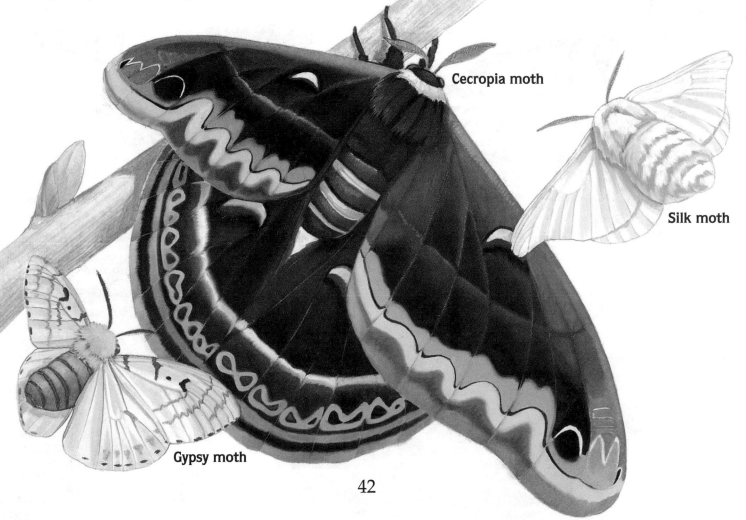

Cecropia moth

Silk moth

Gypsy moth

One of the most important ways insects such as bees and butterflies help us is by aiding *pollination*. As the insects collect the sweet liquid called *nectar* from flowers, they also carry pollen from flower to flower. The pollen makes it possible for the plants to form fruit and new seeds, so more crops and other plants can grow.

Tiger swallowtail

Insects play another important role in nature. They provide food for birds, fish, and other animals.

45

The insect world is alive with fascinating creatures. Carefully watch the insects where you live. Observe their habits, their habitats, and how they look. You're sure to discover a lot about the big world of these small creatures!

Index

abdomen, 14, 15, 39
antennae, 13, 14, 15
ants, 11, 17, 18–19, 29
    females, 19
    males, 19
    nurse, 18, 19
    queen, 18, 19
    soldier, 18, 19
    worker, 19
aphids, 41

bees, 17, 29, 43; *see also* honeybees
beetles, 22, 23, 29
birds, 44
blue night butterfly, 38
boxelder bug, 27
brood, 29
butterflies, 6, 11, 29, 31–38, 43
    adult, 31, 34, 35
    egg, 31, 36
    larva, 31, 32
    pupa, 31, 33
    wings of, 34
    see also monarch butterfly

cabbage butterfly, 38
capped cell, 29, 30
Carolina locust, 22
caterpillars, 31, 32, 33, 36;
    see also monarch caterpillar
Cecropia moth, 42
chinch bugs, 26
chrysalis, 33, 34
cicada, 24–25
    wings of, 25
cocoon, 31
colonies, 17, 18, 19, 20
complete metamorphosis, 29
crickets, 22, 26, 28, 40
    adults, 28
    eggs, 28
    males, 40
    nymphs, 28
crops, 41, 43

digging, 10

disease, 23, 41
dragonflies, 11, 26
drones, 20

eggs, 13, 19, 20, 24, 25, 26–27, 28, 29, 30, 31, 36
entomologist, 16
eyes, 14

feelers, *see* antennae
fighting, 7, 22, 23
fireflies, 39
fish, 44
fleas, 9, 41
flies, 41
flowers, 20, 43
flying, 10, 11
food, 19, 22, 31, 44
fruit, 43

giant water bug, 10
grasshoppers, 22, 26, 27
growth, 13, 16
gypsy moth, 42

head, 13, 14, 15
hive, 20, 21
honey, 20, 30
honeybees, 8, 20–21, 30
    females, 20
    males, 20
    metamorphosis of, 30
    queen, 20, 30
    worker, 20, 30
honeycomb, 30
hunting, 7, 19

insects
    activities of, 16
    adults, 24, 25, 26–27, 28, 29, 30, 31, 34, 35
    bodies of, 13, 14–15
    colors and patterns of, 6, 12, 32, 33
    dangers to, 23
    diet of, 16
    habitats of, 16, 46
    habits of, 16, 46
    harmful to people, 41, 42

    helpful to people, 41, 42, 43
    kinds of, 8
    lifespan of, 23
    places found, 8, 11
    role in nature of, 44
    shapes of, 9
    similarities among, 13
    sizes of, 9
    world of, 6, 39, 46
        sights of, 7, 39
        sounds of, 5, 6, 40

Japanese beetles, 41
jaws, 15
jumping, 10

katydid, 8, 12

ladybug, 8, 12
larva, 29, 30, 31, 32, 42
leaves, 12, 32, 33, 36
legs, 10, 13, 14, 15, 21, 33
lice, 41
locusts, 41
lubber grasshopper, 41

mandibles, *see* jaws
mating, 19, 20, 39, 40
mayflies, 26, 27
metamorphosis, 25–27, 29
migration, 35–37
milkweed, 32, 36
molting, 24, 28, 32, 33
monarch butterfly, 32–37
monarch caterpillar, 32–33, 36
mosquitoes, 22, 41
moths, 29, 31, 42
mouth, 14

nectar, 20, 43
North America, 35
nymph, 26–27, 28

oak gall wasp, 7

paper wasp, 29
Pennsylvania firefly, 39
plants, 23, 36, 43
pollen, 21, 30, 43

pollen baskets, 21
pollination, 43
polyphemus moth, 13
potato bug, 22
praying mantis, 8, 12
pupa, 29, 30, 31, 33

rainbow grasshopper, 12
rose weevil, 41

seeds, 43
shell, 13, 24, 28
silk moth, 42
silk thread, 33, 42
skeleton, 13
skin, 25, 32, 33
smelling, 13
social insects, 17–21
spring, 36
stag beetle, 7, 23
stages of growth, 24–34
starvation, 23
struggle for survival, 23
summer, 35
swimming, 10

thorax, 14–15
thread-waisted wasp, 6
tiger swallowtail, 43
touching, 13
trees, 12, 42
tunnels, 18

viceroy, 38

walking stick, 9
wasps, 29
water boatman, 10
water bugs, 11
weather, 23, 35
weevils, 41
white-lined sphinx moth, 31
wings, 10, 13, 14–15, 25, 34, 40
winter, 36
working, 7, 17, 39

zebra longwing, 38
zebra swallowtail, 38